"Shadow Mastery: Discovering Your Deepest Self"

"The Labyrinth of Your Soul: The Path to Inner Discovery & Healing"

What makes you, you? Have you ever felt a stirring deep within from a part of you that perhaps, remains largely unexplored? For example, do you feel as though the true you is always hidden or suppressed in order to navigate through life and adhere to everyone else's expectations of you? As if you parade through life's duties wearing an armour to conform but inside you are lost?

Through life's largely superficial daily grind, do you ever question who you really are within which may differ vastly from your performance in reality? Like there could be a profound story written in the silent spaces between your thoughts and daily actions, waiting to be discovered?

Is there a part of you that is not allowed to surface to help you cope every day or to assist you to perform in the charade of modern life? Is there another different you who is desperately waiting to be released?

If so, this book might be the lantern that lights up those shadowed corridors of your psyche.

"Shadow Mastery" is more than just a book and a journal; it's a compass for your soul, your source, your inner being, your very essence - your non-physical counterpart that makes you, you. As you turn each page, you'll find yourself diving into ancient myths that echo contemporary struggles, aligning body and mind with exercises that release pent-up emotions and learn how to harness the power of sound, visualisation and nature to bring clarity to your personal journey within whilst co-existing in our complex modern world.

Beyond the scenarios that play out in your daily life, you will be able to master the art of decoding your dreams and tune into the intuitive nudges (often referred to as gut instinct or intuition) that guide your decisions. By embracing the exercises, prompts and reflections offered in this guide, you'll not only learn more about yourself but also how to transform challenges into opportunities and mysteries into revelations allowing you to be the very best version of the authentic you.

So, dear soul seeker, prepare your heart and mind. Get ready to traverse the valleys of your emotions, climb the peaks of your highest aspirations and journey through time's tapestry with tales of transformation. As you embark on this voyage, remember: every whisper of your inner self is a note in the symphony of your existence. Pay attention and you'll be able to uncover the intricate harmonies of your soul.

Authors Bio

Ellie and James Richards have been married for over 36 years. Within their combined lifespan of more than 120 years, their journey has covered a multitude of geographical residences from west London in the UK to Florida USA and southern Spain. Along their path together there has been a rollercoaster of events which have included both triumphs and devastation and everything in between. From success to hardship and back again (more than once) with varied and eclectic career paths, emotions have run very high with deep levels of stress and anxiety which they have found hard, if not almost impossible to manage at times.

It has been that rich and highly challenging odyssey that led them to look inward and seek to better control and improve themselves, not only to grow and find inner peace, but also to face demons, past and present and experience life in a more manageable and fruitful way, especially through times of great anxiety, difficulty and sorrow.

Whilst throughout adulthood they have consistently practised healthy living in terms of exercise and nutrition, the mental and emotional side started to beckon and call for more of their attention as the years rolled by and the adverse events unfolded in their lives.

Initially starting with yoga back in the late 90's, including meditation, their interest in the mind later evolved further into the workings of the brain, our emotions, our demons, our fears and exploring coping mechanisms to assist in life's more demanding situations.

By reading and listening to highly insightful and inspirational people from Dr. Joe Dispenza and Dr. Bruce Lipton to motivational speakers like Tony Robbins and Dr. Wayne Dyer to the ancients like Rumi and Marcus Aurelius, to name but a few, their interest, understanding and perspective about humanity and our very souls has flourished and become part of their daily lives.

Ellie and James continue to practise all of these today and the wisdom from their shared journey, ripe with tales of trials and triumphs, has been distilled into these pages. As you embark on this transformative exploration, remember you are not just reading a book; you are diving into a combined century's worth of worldly wisdom, plus lessons from ancient myths and helpful practices and profound introspections that have shaped their own inner beings. It is their earnest intention that it will help the reader in their own personal journey to inner discovery, healing and ultimate peace.

Welcome to 'Shadow Mastery'.

With warmest regards and deepest reverence

Ellie and James Richards

Disclaimer

This book, "Shadow Mastery – Discover your Deeper Self" and its contents, hereafter referred to as "the Book," is intended for informational and educational purposes only. It should not be construed as offering medical, psychological, therapeutic, or any other form of professional advice. All concepts, techniques, and advice mentioned in the Book are based on the personal experiences, opinions and research of the authors and are shared in good faith. The results described in the Book may vary from person to person and there is no guarantee, promise or warranty that reading or applying the advice or techniques mentioned in the Book will produce the same results for everyone.

While the Book references various methodologies like Yoga, Tai Chi, Qigong and Meditation, it does not assert the effectiveness or suitability of these techniques for every individual or situation. Users of this Book should consult with a qualified health professional regarding any potential physical or mental health concerns before embarking on any new therapeutic methods or techniques mentioned herein.

The authors and publisher disclaim responsibility for any adverse effects or consequences resulting directly or indirectly from the use or misuse of the Book's contents, or from any actions or decisions taken based on the information provided.

Always seek the guidance of a qualified professional in the relevant field when considering changes to your health, lifestyle or mental well-being. The Book is not a substitute for individual therapy, medical advice or professional counselling. By continuing to read or utilise the information in this Book, the reader accepts full responsibility for any outcome or consequence and agrees to hold the authors, publisher and all affiliated parties harmless from any claims, complaints or legal actions.

Any references to third-party sources, products, services or websites do not imply endorsement and the authors and publisher are not responsible for the content or reliability of any linked information or third-party services.

Contents

INTRODUCTION

In the grand tapestry of human existence, each individual is a unique thread, weaving a story of experiences, emotions, dreams and realities. It's easy to get lost in the humdrum of daily existence, forgetting that beneath the roles we play and the masks we wear, lies an ocean of a much deeper self, often suppressed or unexplored.

During every era and across multiple cultures, stories have been told of heroes embarking on quests, navigating labyrinths or scaling mountains to find a hidden treasure. These aren't just mythical tales of adventure but are metaphors of the human journey. A quest into the heart of our own personal labyrinth, where the treasure isn't a chest of gold but the golden discovery of the truth of our inner self. It's this journey that *"The Labyrinth of Your Soul: The Path to Inner Discovery & Healing"* invites you on.

Imagine, for a moment, a diary that belonged to one of your great-grandparents. Between its worn-out pages, you'd find not just dates and events, but emotions, secrets and aspirations. Each entry would be a window into their soul, a chapter of a life lived long before you existed. Now consider this: generations from now, someone might hold your diary, exploring the depths of who you were. What stories would it tell? What emotions would echo through time in your life?

As Jack Canfield once said,

"Everything you want is on the other side of fear."

Our deepest fears, insecurities and shadows are not barriers but bridges. Bridges that lead us to the richest parts of our soul, the parts that hold our strength, wisdom and individuality.

This book isn't just a read; it's an experience. Through various sections, you'll engage with activities and introspections, myths and tales, sounds and silences. The goal is not just self-awareness but also self-celebration. It's about illuminating the darkest corners of your psyche, dancing with your shadows and letting them lead you to the light.

Perhaps you're wondering why embark on this journey? To that, I'd share a memory. I remember sitting with my grandmother, a woman of great wisdom, listening to her tales of youth. Amidst stories of struggles and joys, she'd often say,

"To know the world, you must first know yourself."

A common saying back then but in understanding our fears, dreams, strengths and vulnerabilities, we don't just become better individuals but also more compassionate members of human society.

As you dive into this book, remember that each section is a steppingstone, each activity and introspection a note in the orchestra of your soul. Take your time, revisit sections when needed and let the journey shape you as much as you shape it.

The world outside is a reflection of the world within. And as you stand at the threshold of this inner expedition, remember the words of the ancient Chinese philosopher Laozi:

"Knowing others is wisdom, knowing yourself is enlightenment."

Let this be your odyssey and your enlightenment. Welcome to the personal labyrinth of your own essence and let your discovery begin.

Please bear in mind that some parts of this book and its various contents and exercises may resonate more than others. Allow yourself the space to embrace each one when you feel the timing is right and omit any that don't. Remember, there is no right or wrong with any of this. It is for you to find your way. Bon voyage!

1. Dynamic Inner Exploration Tasks - Begin the journey with engaging activities.

2. Collection of 60 Thought-Provoking Diary Prompts - A series of introspective prompts.

3. Mythological Reflections: Understanding Our Shadows Through Timeless Tales - Connect ancient stories to present struggles.

4. Body and Shadow: Physical Exercises for Emotional Release - Connecting physical wellness and emotional wellbeing.

5. Meditative Soundscapes: Using Sound to Dive Deeper - Integrating auditory senses to introspection.

6. Archetypal Journeys: Identifying the Characters Within - Recognizing recurring patterns in life.

7. Dreamscapes and the Subconscious - Introducing the mystique and revelations of dreams.

8. Emotional Ecosystems - A detailed exploration of emotions and their interrelations.

9. Art of Visualisation - Empowering the imagination as a tool for self-discovery.

10. Blank Canvas Sections - A space for free expression and personal reflection.

11. Conclusion and Further Resources - Wrapping up the journey and pointing towards more resources for exploration.

1

Dynamic Inner Exploration Tasks

The human psyche is a vast and complex ocean, teeming with untold mysteries, vibrant corals of emotion and occasionally, haunting shadows of the past. Plunging into this ocean might seem daunting, but it's an essential journey for anyone seeking true self-awareness. Let's embark together on this voyage of discovery using a series of tasks designed to illuminate every hidden corner of your inner self.

1. Personal Timeline Creation:

Description: Craft a timeline of your life, marking significant events, both positive and negative.

Purpose: To visually see the ebb and flow of experiences in your life, providing clarity on phases of growth, stagnation or regression.

Reflection: Looking at the timeline, are there patterns that emerge? Periods of rapid growth or decline?

____

____

____

____

____

2. The Emotional Palette:

Description: Visualise your emotions as colours. Assign a colour to each feeling and create an "emotional painting" reflecting the past month.

Purpose: This exercise assists in recognizing and naming emotions, making them tangible.

Reflection: Which colours dominate? Are there surprising shades that have emerged? Are they troublingly dark or more vibrant and lighter? What do you conclude from this?

____

____

____

____

____

3. Conversations with the Past:

Description: Write a letter to your 10-year-old self. Offer advice and comfort or simply share an update about life.

Purpose: To build compassion for your past self and recognize the journey undertaken.

Reflection: What were the primary concerns at that age? How have they evolved to your current self?

____

____

____

____

____

4. Core Belief Identification:

Description: List out beliefs you hold about the world, yourself and others. Challenge each belief by asking, "Why do I believe this?"

Purpose: Unearthing foundational beliefs can unveil behaviours and emotional reactions.

Reflection: Which beliefs empower you? Which ones do you feel limit you?

____

____

____

____

____

5. Body Scan Meditation:

Description: Sit or lie down in a quiet space. Mentally scan your body from head to toe, noticing any sensations, tensions or discomfort.

Purpose: Ground yourself in the present and understand how emotions can manifest physically.

Reflection: Are there areas of consistent tension? Could these be linked to emotional distress or past traumas?

____

____

____

____

6. Fear Facing:

Description: List out your top five fears. For each fear, describe a scenario where it comes true. Then, outline steps for recovery or coping with it.

Purpose: Confronting fears reduces their control over you and equips you with coping strategies.

Reflection: Are there common themes in your fears? How realistic are they? Could you be unnecessarily catastrophising?

____

____

____

____

____

7. Achievement Audit:

Description: Catalogue your achievements, both big and small. Celebrate them.

Purpose: Fosters self-worth and recognizes growth areas.

Reflection: Which achievements make you proudest and why?

____

____

____

____

____

8. Roleplay:

Description: List out the roles you play in life (parent, employee, friend, etc.). Choose one and write about a day in that role.

Purpose: Understand the expectations and pressures of each role.

Reflection: Which roles are most fulfilling? Which are most challenging?

____

____

____

____

9. Mask Making:

Description: Artistically create masks that represent different facets of your personality. You can draw or paint them or even make them.

Purpose: To acknowledge the different personas we adopt in various scenarios.

Reflection: Are there masks you wish you could shed? And any you wish you could wear more often?

____

____

____

____

____

10. The Gratitude Journal:

Description: Daily, jot down three things you're thankful for. This can be anything from sunshine to your pet. It doesn't have to be a big thing.

Purpose: Fosters positivity and shifts your focus from lack to abundance.

Reflection: Over time, do themes emerge in your areas of gratitude?

____

____

____

____

____

These tasks are but the first steps in our exploration. As you engage with each task, ensure you do so with an open heart and mind. Set aside judgement and allow authentic emotions to flow. You don't have to do all of them. If any of them feel daunting or make you uncomfortable - leave them for now.

Each task, reflection and insight will pave the way towards a more profound understanding of your intricate psyche.

To enhance the exploration further, we'll weave in stories from various individuals who embarked on similar inner quests.

Anecdote - Sarah's Personal Timeline:

When Sarah charted her life, she was stunned to notice a pattern. Every three years, she seemed to undergo a significant change - a new job, a new relationship or a big move. Recognising this pattern, she could then anticipate and prepare for significant shifts, making transitions smoother. In simple terms it heightened her awareness and intuition.

Anecdote - Raj's Emotional Palette:

For Raj, anger was always present and a red, bright, blazing crimson. But when he looked deeper, he recognised hues of pink - hinting at the hurt beneath the anger. This realisation transformed his conflict resolution approach.

By intertwining such real-life experiences with tasks, we offer not just a theoretical approach but a lived experience, making the journey of introspection both relatable and deeply personal.

2

Collection of 60 Thought-Provoking Diary Prompts

1. Personal Universe:

If your mind were a galaxy, what would its planets represent? Describe these celestial bodies and their significance in your inner cosmos.

____

____

____

____

____

2. The Mask We Wear:

Recall a moment when you wore a 'mask' to fit into a situation. How did it feel and what truths did it hide?

____

____

____

____

3. Life's Soundtrack:

Imagine your life is a movie. What song plays during its most memorable scene? Why this track?

____

____

____

____

____

4. The Crossroads:

Describe a pivotal decision point in your life. What other path could you have taken, and where might it have led?

____

____

____

____

5. Legacy Letters:

If you were to write a letter to future generations, what wisdom or cautionary tales would it hold?

____

____

____

____

____

6. Dream Realms:

Recall a memorable dream. Dive deep into its symbols and emotions. What might they signify?

____

____

____

____

____

7. Emotional Landscapes:

If emotions were tangible landscapes, how would joy, sorrow, anger and love appear to you? Describe or draw their terrains.

____

____

____

8. Wisdom from Mistakes:

Think of a mistake in your life as if it were a teacher. What's the
most significant lesson you've learned from one of your errors?

____

____

____

____

____

9. Philosophical Musing:

"If life is a question, what is its answer?" Ponder on this and
detail your reflections.

____

____

____

____

____

10. Life without Filters:

In an age of social media, describe a raw, unfiltered moment of
your life that you've never shared.

____

____

____

____

11. Time's Echo:

If you could send a message to your younger self, what would you say?

____

____

____

____

12. The Tides of Time:

How have your perceptions of success and happiness evolved over the years?

____

____

____

____

13. Meeting the Shadow:

Imagine meeting a side of you that you've always ignored or denied. What would it look like? What would it say?

____

____

____

____

____

14. In Another's Shoes:

Think of someone you've judged harshly or misunderstood. Rewrite a chapter of their life story from their perspective.

____

____

____

____

____

15. Unsung Melodies:

What's a silent passion or talent you have that most people don't know about? Why have you kept it quiet?

____

____

____

16. Uncharted Destinations:

If you could journey to an unexplored part of your psyche, what do you think you'd find there?

____

____

____

____

____

17. Ethical Mirrors:

Recall a moral dilemma you faced. If you had chosen differently, how might your life have diverged?

____

____

____

____

____

18. The Storyteller:

If your life were a book, what would its title be? Then write its blurb.

____

____

____

____

____

19. Cosmic Significance:

Ponder on your role in the universe. In its vast expanse, where do you feel you fit in?

____

____

____

____

____

20. Love's Spectrum:

Love manifests in various forms. Describe an unconventional form of love you've either experienced or witnessed.

____

____

____

____

____

21. The Silent Observer:

As a silent observer of your life, what patterns or habits stand out? Why might they have developed?

____

____

____

____

____

22. Forgotten Fragments:

Recollect a nearly forgotten memory from childhood. Why do you think it surfaced now?

____

____

____

____

____

23. Nature's Lessons:

Nature teaches silently. Describe a lesson you've learned from observing the natural world.

____

____

____

24. The Book of Regrets:

If regrets were chapters in a book, which one would be its most poignant tale in your life?

____

____

____

____

____

25. Dialogue with Despair:

If you could converse with your despair or anxiety, what questions would you ask? How might they reply?

____

____

____

____

____

26. Life's Paintbrush:

Imagine your life as a canvas. What colours dominate? Are there any you wish to introduce or erase?

____

____

____

____

____

27. Echoes of Laughter:

When was the last time you laughed so hard your belly hurt? Delve into that moment's joy and write down what it was and how it felt.

____

____

____

____

____

28. The Wisdom Well:

If you had a well that held answers, what would you ask it today?

____

____

____

____

____

29. The Future's Gaze:

How do you imagine your future self? Write a letter to them detailing your hopes and fears.

____

____

____

____

____

30. Values Vault:

List your core values. Choose one and describe a moment when it was challenged.

____

____

____

____

31. The Dance of Time:

If time were a dance, what steps has it taught you?

____

____

____

____

____

32. Night's Whispers:

Night holds a special magic. Describe a nocturnal memory that has stayed with you.

____

____

____

____

____

33. Joy's Recipe:

What are the ingredients of your joy? How can you cultivate more of them?

____

____

____

____

____

34. Inner Landmarks:

Just as cities have landmarks, our minds have pivotal memories. What are your inner landmarks?

____

____

____

____

____

35. The Theatre of Thoughts:

Your mind is a theatre. What play is it currently staging?

____

____

____

____

36. Life's Unsolved Mysteries:

What's one question about life you've always pondered but never found an answer to?

____

____

____

____

37. Your Anthem:

If your spirit had an anthem, what would its lyrics be?

____

____

____

____

____

38. The Silent Scream:

What's something you've always wanted to shout from the rooftops but held back? Why?

____

____

____

____

39. The Compass of Morality:

Describe a time when your moral compass pointed you in a surprising direction.

____

____

____

____

____

40. The Garden of Gratitude:

If gratitude were flowers, which one's bloom most often in your garden?

____

____

____

____

____

41. Forgotten Dreams:

Think of a dream or aspiration you had but set aside. What made you leave it behind?

____

____

____

____

____

42. The Symphony of Solitude:

How does solitude sound to you? Is it a soothing melody or a haunting echo?

____

____

____

____

____

43. Emotional Alchemy:

Describe an emotion you'd like to transform. How would you go about it?

____

____

____

____

____

44. The Map of Beliefs:

Chart out your core beliefs. Which ones have shifted over the years and why?

____

____

____

____

45. The Gallery of Faces:

Think of the people who've impacted your life. Paint a mental portrait of one such individual.

____

____

____

____

____

46. The Language of Silence:

When was a moment that silence spoke louder than words? Describe its eloquence and the ensuing result.

____

____

____

____

____

47. The Vault of Vulnerability:

Detail a moment of vulnerability. How did it transform you, your circumstance or your relationships?

____

____

____

____

____

48. The Echo of Euphoria:

Recall an instance of pure euphoria. Dive deep into its essence.

____

____

____

____

____

49. Footprints in the Sands of Time:

What legacy do you want to leave behind in the vast sands of time?

____

____

____

____

____

50. The Web of Interconnectedness:

Contemplate on how your actions ripple outwards. Describe a ripple effect you've observed.

____

____

____

____

51. The River of Resilience:

Life flows like a river. Describe a time it tested your resilience.
How did you navigate its currents?

____

____

____

____

52. The Fires of Passion:

What sets your soul on fire? Describe this passion and its origin.

____

____

____

____

53. The Shadow's Embrace:

Recount a time when embracing a shadow aspect of yourself led to enlightenment.

____

____

____

____

____

54. The Cosmic Conversation:

If you could converse with the universe, what would you ask? What do you think it might reply?

____

____

____

____

____

55. The Labyrinth of Choices:

Life presents countless paths. Describe a time you stood at a crossroads, uncertain of the way forward.

____

____

____

56. The Mirror of Memories:

Memories mirror our past. Reflect on a memory you'd revisit if given a chance. Why?

____

____

____

____

57. The Ode to Optimism:

Write an ode to optimism, capturing its essence and significance in your life.

____

____

____

____

58. The Dance with Darkness:

Darkness isn't always ominous. Describe a time when dancing with darkness brought about clarity for you.

59. The Beacon of Belonging:

Belonging can be a beacon in the fog of loneliness. Describe a moment of feeling a profound sense of belonging.

____

____

____

____

____

60. The Odyssey of the Self:

Life is an odyssey. Where are you in your journey and where do you aspire to go?

____

____

____

____

Conclusion to Diary Prompts:

The essence of introspection often lies in the questions we ask ourselves. These prompts are designed not just as questions, but to act as markers reflecting the myriad facets of your core being. As you pen your responses, understand that there are no right or wrong answers. The value lies in the process of exploration and the insights that emerge. Embrace this journey and let each prompt be a steppingstone toward deeper self-awareness. You may even notice a common theme or pattern since many of the questions are interconnected.

3

MYTHOLOGICAL REFLECTIONS: UNDERSTANDING OUR SHADOWS THROUGH TIMELESS TALES

The annals of mythology are more than mere tales; they are ageless echoes of humanity's dreams, fears, hopes and desires. For centuries, these stories have captivated us, not just because of their fantastical elements, but often due to their uncanny reflection of our own experiences. In this age of rapid change and evolving societal norms, mythology offers an unbroken mirror to the soul, a compass pointing the way to deeper introspection.

Icarus and the Lure of Ambition

One of the most poignant Greek myths is that of Icarus, who, with wings made of feathers and wax, flew too close to the sun. Despite his father's warning, the intoxicating allure of the skies proved too much, causing the wax to melt and Icarus to plummet into the sea.

In today's world, ambition drives many of us. We're told to aim high, to break the mould, to achieve the impossible. Yet, the tale of Icarus reminds us of the potential dangers of unchecked ambition. How often do we push ourselves too far, ignoring the warnings, until we face our own downfall?

Reflection:

Are there areas in your life where ambition blinds you to potential perils? How can you achieve balance, ensuring your drive doesn't lead to your downfall?

____

____

____

____

____

Pandora and the Shadow of Curiosity

"Behind every choice is a consequence, behind every curiosity is a revelation."

When Pandora opened her forbidden box, she unleashed all the evils into the world, leaving only hope trapped within. This myth reveals the duality of curiosity – a force that can lead to both discovery and despair.

Every day, we are faced with our own "boxes" – decisions, opportunities and choices that incite our curiosity. The story compels us to question: When does curiosity enrich us and when does it endanger us? In an age of limitless information, the Pandora myth begs the question: How do we filter our curiosities? Do we open every box? Or do we choose wisely, understanding that not all revelations are beneficial?

Reflection:

Think of a time when your curiosity led you down an unexpected path. What evils and hopes did it release? How did it shape your journey of self-awareness?

____

____

____

____

____

Narcissus and the Search for Self-Love

"To see oneself clearly is an art; to love oneself is a journey."

Narcissus, entranced by his reflection, symbolises the pitfalls of excessive self-adoration. But in the modern age, where self-image and validation often come from external sources like social media, this myth definitely invites a deeper exploration.

Today's struggle isn't just about vanity; it's about understanding the difference between self-love and self-obsession. Where does healthy self-appreciation end and destructive narcissism begin?

Reflection:

How do you perceive yourself? Do external validations define your self-worth? How can you cultivate genuine self-love and of being your authentic self without falling into the trap of narcissism or letting your outer appearance become the all-important factor in your life?

____

____

____

____

____

Odysseus and the Sirens: Facing Temptation

"In the melody of temptation, find your anchor in wisdom."

Odysseus, on his long voyage home, knew that he'd encounter the mesmerising songs of the Sirens. To protect himself, he filled his crew's ears with wax and had himself tied to the mast. This way, he could experience the allure without yielding to it.

The sirens' song is a metaphor for life's many temptations. In an era of instant gratification, this tale underscores the importance of foresight, preparation and self-restraint.

Reflection:

What are the "siren songs" in your life? How do you prepare yourself to face these temptations without succumbing? Temptations abound, but foresight and self-awareness can guide us safely past them. Remember, knowing your weaknesses is a strength; it allows preparation and, ultimately, mastery over temptations.

____

____

____

____

____

The Phoenix: Resilience and Rebirth

"From the ashes, we rise. In every ending, there's a promise of a new beginning."

The legend of the Phoenix, a bird that regenerates from its ashes, symbolises the cycle of destruction and rebirth. It embodies the power of resilience, transformation and the undying human spirit when the odds are seemingly stacked against us.

Today, many of us face our own metaphorical fires – trials that test our mettle. But like the Phoenix, we too possess the innate ability to rise again, transform and begin anew. There's much wisdom in the old saying "Pick yourself up, dust yourself down and start all over again."

Reflection:

Recall a moment of significant challenge in your life. How did you emerge from it? What did you learn and how did you transform?

____

____

____

____

____

The Minotaur and the Labyrinth: Facing Our Inner Demons

"Every heart has its labyrinth, every soul, its Minotaur. The journey isn't about escaping but confronting."

In the heart of the Labyrinth lurked the Minotaur, a terrifying creature. It wasn't just a monster but a manifestation of fear, guilt and shame. Theseus, with Ariadne's help, confronted this monster, weaving a path through the complexities of the maze.

Today, we all have our internal labyrinths — intricate paths of past regrets, fears and insecurities. Avoidance is but a temporary respite. True liberation comes from confronting our Minotaur, facing our innermost fears and challenges.

Reflection:

What are the walls of your personal labyrinth made of? Is there a Minotaur you've been avoiding? With courage and support, confronting these challenges can lead to profound transformation, release and self-awareness.

____

____

____

____

____

Hercules and His Twelve Labours: The Path of Redemption

"Every challenge, no matter how Herculean, holds a lesson. In overcoming, we find our true self."

For his transgressions, Hercules had to perform twelve seemingly impossible tasks. Each labour wasn't just a physical challenge but also a moral and spiritual test. In facing these challenges, Hercules not only found redemption but also self-realisation.

Our life journey is peppered with challenges — our own set of 'labours.' Some we choose; others are thrust upon us. Yet, in each challenge lies an opportunity for growth, learning and improvement.

Reflection:

Look back on your 'labours' in life. The moments that really tested your spirit and resolve. Were they not the instances that also shaped you, taught you invaluable lessons and redefined you as a result of your achievements in difficult circumstances?

Orpheus and Eurydice: Letting Go with Love

"Sometimes, the most profound act of love is letting go."

Orpheus's love for Eurydice was so profound that he journeyed into the underworld for her. But he was warned not to look back until they reached the mortal realm. Moments away from success, doubt plagued him and he turned, losing Eurydice forever.

This tale touches the very essence of human vulnerability. Trust, faith and the art of letting go are central to our life's journey. Sometimes, our fears and insecurities cause us to falter at the very brink of success.

Reflection:

Ponder over moments when doubt crept in, moments when you hesitated and looked back. Can you recognise the beauty in surrender, in trusting and moving forward without fear and constantly needing to look back?

The Lotus Eaters: The Seduction of Complacency

"Comfort can be an elixir, but also a chain."

Odysseus's men, upon eating the fruit of the Lotus plant, lost all desire for change or progress, wanting only to linger in their present state of contentment. This tale is a timeless reminder of the perils of becoming too comfortable or losing sight of one's goals.

Today, we often encounter our lotus fruits – be it a complacent job, a stagnant relationship or any other type of comfort zone that keeps us from evolving and pursuing our dreams.

Reflection:

What are your 'lotus fruits'? Those things that keep you tethered, preventing expansion, new opportunities and experiences. Remember, life isn't just about comfort but about growth, evolution and the pursuit of one's true potential.

Demeter and Persephone: Seasons of the Soul

"Every heart has its winters and springs; every soul, its seasons of darkness and light."

Persephone's descent into the underworld and the resulting seasons mirror the ebb and flow in our lives. The cold of winter, the bloom of spring — life is a dance of shadows and light, of chill and warmth.

In our lives, moments of despair are often followed by times of elation, like seasons following a set rhythm. Embracing this cyclical nature helps us understand that after periods of darkness, light invariably follows. Nothing lasts forever and everything passes.

Reflection:

Reflect on your life's seasons. The winters of despair, the springs of hope. Can you see the pattern, the rhythm and the promise that every winter will eventually give way to spring?

____

____

____

____

____

These myths, though ancient, resonate deeply even today. They aren't just tales; they're reflections, echoes of our struggles, dreams, fears and hopes. As we journey through life, let these stories guide us, reminding us of the timeless lessons woven into our very essence. Embrace these tales, for within them lie keys to understanding our deepest selves.

4

Body and Shadow: Physical Exercises for Emotional Release

Our bodies serve as living testimonies to our emotional experiences. Often, the weight of our shadows – those unresolved conflicts, suppressed emotions and hidden fears – manifest in our physical form. It could be the tension in our shoulders, the slump of our posture, the pain in our lower backs and hips or the constriction in our chest.

The Connection Between Emotion and Motion:

Before we dive into specific exercises, it's crucial to understand the intrinsic link between emotion and motion. When we experience intense emotion – be it anger, sadness, joy or fear – our body reacts in kind. For instance, when frightened, our body tenses up, ready for the "fight or flight" response. On the flip side, a good bout of laughter can relax our muscles for up to 45 minutes afterward! There's much truth in the old saying "Laughter is the best medicine."

By being mindful of our body and using intentional physical exercises, we can address emotional knots, release pent-up emotions and even foster positive feelings.

Just like the mystical tales of old in the previous chapter, many of these come from ancient practices and beliefs in the form of yoga, tai chi and qi gong.

Try the below ancient ways of movement for release, restoring balance, reducing anxiety and inner focus.

Important to note that if you have any physical pain that any of these poses and movements enhance then please refrain. The idea is to heal not harm.

1. Grounding with Mountain Pose:

- ***Physical Execution:***

  Stand tall with feet hip-width apart, arms by your side, with the crown of your head reaching towards the sky. Feel your feet rooted firmly to the ground as you breathe deeply, inhaling through your nose, allowing each exhale to further ground you.

- ***Symbolic Meaning:***

  This pose signifies strength, stability and grounding. Just as a mountain stands tall, unwavering against the forces of nature, Tadasana teaches us to find stability and strength in our lives.

- ***Emotional Release:*** As you immerse yourself in the pose, imagine shedding layers of stress, anxiety and doubt. This pose allows for a profound emotional grounding, centering the mind and calming turbulent emotions.

2. **Releasing Frustration with Shadow Boxing:**

- ***Physical Execution:***

  Adopt a fighter's stance with feet shoulder-width apart, one foot slightly ahead of the other. Ball your hands into fists, protecting your face. Proceed to throw punches (jabs, crosses, hooks) into the air, imagining an opponent or a shadow.

- ***Symbolic Meaning:***

  The act of boxing with one's shadow embodies the confrontation with inner demons, fears and frustrations. It's about taking control and finding rhythm amidst chaos.

- ***Emotional Release:***

  With each punch, visualise releasing pent-up emotions. The faster, rhythmic movements act as a cathartic release of stress, anger and any emotional baggage bearing down on you.

3. **Embracing Vulnerability with Child's Pose:**

- ***Physical Execution:***

  Start by kneeling on the floor, then lean forward, extending your arms in front of you and resting your forehead on the ground. Breathe deeply through the nose, feeling the stretch across your back.

- ***Symbolic Meaning:***

  Returning to a foetal position, this pose is reminiscent of our time in the womb—safe, nurtured and protected. It symbolises surrender, humility and a return to one's inner being.

- ***Emotional Release:***

  As you fold into yourself, this pose encourages introspection, allowing one to release feelings of vulnerability, fear and resistance, creating a safe space to embrace and process these emotions.

4. **Unlocking Tension with Neck Rolls:**

- ***Physical Execution:***

  Sit or stand comfortably. Slowly tilt your head to one side, roll it gently to the front and then to the other side, forming a half or full circle, based on your comfort.

- ***Symbolic Meaning:***

  The neck, a bridge between the head (mind) and the body, often bears the weight of unspoken words and unexpressed feelings. Neck rolls signify the unburdening of this weight and the release of suppressed tensions.

- ***Emotional Release:***

  With each rotation, imagine letting go of repressed emotions, unsaid words or pent-up frustrations. The gentle movement can be both a physical and emotional release, offering relief and lightness.

5. The Butterfly Hug:

- ***Physical Execution:***

  Sit comfortably, cross your arms over your chest so your hands rest on your upper arms. Tap one hand then the other, alternating in a rhythm that feels natural to you. Breathe deeply through the nose as you tap.

- ***Symbolic Meaning:***

  This technique, often used in trauma therapy, mimics the motion of a butterfly's wings. The butterfly undergoes a profound transformation in its life, changing from caterpillar to winged beauty. Like the butterfly, we too can transform our pains and traumas into growth and freedom.

- ***Emotional Release:***

  The rhythmic tapping can help in grounding, calming the nervous system and alleviating traumatic memories.

6. The Tree Pose Rebalance:

- ***Physical Execution:***

  Stand on one foot, placing the sole of the other foot on the inside of the standing leg, either below the knee or above it, forming a tree pose. Extend your arms upwards, palms touching if possible, looking forward or closing your eyes. Balance and breathe deeply through your nose. If holding your arms up is difficult, place them in a prayer position at your heart.

- ***Symbolic Meaning:***

  Trees are grounded, yet they reach for the sky. They experience seasons, growth and renewal. Emulating a tree, you're grounding your experiences and reaching for growth.

- ***Emotional Release:***

  Helps in fostering a sense of balance, grounding and connection to the earth. It can assist in moments when you feel emotionally overwhelmed or disconnected.

7. Emotional Release through Dance:

- ***Physical Execution:***

  Play a piece of instrumental music that resonates with your current emotional state. Without choreography, allow your body to move to the rhythm and beats, expressing your emotions through movement.

- ***Symbolic Meaning:***

  Dance has been a form of expression for aeons. It's a primal, uninhibited way of connecting with one's emotions, past and desires.

- ***Emotional Release:***

  Dance provides an outlet for bottled-up feelings, giving them form and motion, aiding in their release and encouraging freedom. When you do this by yourself with no judgement from others about what you look like, it can be wonderfully liberating.

8. The Heart-Opening Bridge Pose:

- ***Physical Execution:***

  Lie on your back. Bend your knees and place your feet flat on the ground about hips width apart. Press your palms down with your fingers pointing towards your heels. Lift your body upwards from your pelvis, arching your back. Hold for a few breaths and release.

- ***Symbolic Meaning:***

  This posture opens up the chest area, symbolising vulnerability and openness. It's a powerful gesture of trusting the universe with your heart.

- ***Emotional Release:***

  It can help in letting go of protective barriers around the heart, releasing past hurts and fostering openness to new experiences.

9.Power in Plank Pose:

- ***Physical Execution:***

  Begin in a push-up position, hands under the shoulders. Engage your core and hold the position, ensuring your body forms a straight line from head to heel.

- ***Symbolic Meaning:***

  Holding the plank is about endurance and resilience. It represents the strength required to face life's challenges and adversities.

- ***Emotional Release:***

  In this challenging pose, focus on your breath, breathing deeply through your nose and tap into any buried feelings of inadequacy or doubt. As you hold, imagine drawing strength and resilience, expelling any negative feelings with each exhale.

10. Tai-Chi:

- ***Physical Execution:***

Start by standing in a relaxed position. Engage in a series of slow, flowing body movements that transition seamlessly from one to the next. See the basic flow diagram for guidance.

- ***Symbolic Meaning:***

Tai Chi is often called "meditation in motion." It represents balance, harmony and the eternal dance between yin and yang.

- ***Emotional Release:***

As you glide through movements, allow Tai Chi to calm your mind, releasing stress, anxiety and daily pressures, welcoming peace and clarity.

11. Stretching Beyond with Sun Salutations:

- ***Physical Execution:***

  Begin standing upright, then flow through the series of poses including forward bend, plank, cobra, down dog, etc., as per the diagrams, eventually returning to the standing position.

- ***Symbolic Meaning:***

  Sun Salutations are a tribute to the life-giving sun. They symbolise a fresh start, the dawning of a new day and the endless cycle of life and rebirth.

- ***Emotional Release:***

  Use this flow to release stagnation, greet the new day with hope and let go of past regrets or worries about the future.

12. Channelling Energy with Qi Gong:

- ***Physical Execution:***

  Engage in a combination of rhythmic breathing, fluid movement and meditation. Feel the flow of Qi (energy) within. Use the images below to guide you.

- ***Symbolic Meaning:***

  Qi Gong taps into the ancient Chinese concept of life force. It symbolises the harnessing and harmonising of one's energy.

- ***Emotional Release:***

  This practice can help dispel emotional blockages, promoting a sense of calm, balance and a revitalised energy.

Strength in Warrior Pose:

- ***Physical Execution:***

  Standing, step one foot back, bend the front knee, and stretch your arms apart, one forward and one back fixing your gaze ahead at your middle finger level. See the image below for guidance.

- ***Symbolic Meaning:***

  The Warrior Pose signifies strength, courage and determination. It's a celebration of the warrior spirit within each of us.

- ***Emotional Release:***

  Use this pose to summon your inner strength, confront fears, and face challenges head-on.

Flexibility in Bow Pose:

- ***Physical Execution:***

  Lying on your stomach, reach back to grasp your ankles, lifting your chest and thighs off the ground.

- ***Symbolic Meaning:***

  Bow Pose represents flexibility and opening up. It's about bending but not breaking.

- ***Emotional Release:***

  Use this pose to release feelings of rigidity or resistance, embracing flexibility and adaptability.

Restorative Release with Deep Breathing:

- ***Physical Execution:***

  Sit comfortably. Take a deep inhale through the nose, feeling your belly expand, then exhale deeply through the mouth.

- ***Symbolic Meaning:***

  Deep breathing is about life force. Each breath nourishes the body and spirit, signifying the cyclical nature of life and rejuvenation.

- ***Emotional Release:***

  Let go of stress and tension, using each exhale to release negativity and each inhale to draw in peace and positivity.

Gazing Within with Candle Meditation:

- ***Physical Execution:***

  Sit comfortably, placing a lit candle at eye level. Softly gaze at the flame, letting all other thoughts fade.

- ***Symbolic Meaning:***

  The flame is a beacon of clarity and insight. This meditation represents inner light and wisdom.

- ***Emotional Release:***

  By focusing solely on the flame, it allows you to let go of external distractions and find clarity amidst emotional chaos.

Grounded Thoughts with Seated Meditation:

- ***Physical Execution:***

  Sit comfortably, spine straight. Close your eyes and focus on your breath or a chosen mantra. (More on mantras later)

- ***Symbolic Meaning:***

  Seated meditation is a return to the self. It represents introspection, stillness and grounding amidst life's whirlwinds.

- ***Emotional Release:***

  Dive deep within, letting go of external worries and finding peace within the stillness of your own being.

Each of these exercises is a tool and an avenue for understanding and processing the vast emotional landscape within. Through movement and stillness alike, they offer a gateway to emotional clarity and catharsis.

By exploring these movements, you will discover the ones that serve you best and be able to revisit them when life creates stress and anxiety. Regular practice is advised for optimal results.

NOTE:

Yoga, Tai Chi, Qi Gong, mediation and breathwork all have their own distinct benefits and there are vast resources available both in the written word, videos and classes which we would encourage you to explore further.

5

MEDITATIVE SOUNDSCAPES: USING SOUND TO DIVE DEEPER

"In the symphony of life, every note, every silence and every resonance tell a story. Listening attentively can be the gateway to profound self-awareness."

The beauty of existence is that it sings. From the gentle rustling of autumn leaves to the rhythmic cadence of our heartbeats, life is an orchestra of sounds. These sounds, often overlooked in the chaos of everyday life, have the power to lead us deeper within, unveiling layers of our consciousness previously untouched.

The Essence of Sound in Introspection

Have you ever sat by the ocean, letting the sound of the waves' ebb and flow wash over you and resonate within, perhaps summoning memories, emotions and reflections? Or perhaps felt the quiet hum of chanting or a bird song that stirs something within? This is the magic of sound.

Sound is a direct channel to our subconscious mind. Unlike our other senses, which process stimuli more consciously, auditory senses can bypass cognitive barriers and directly affect our emotional and spiritual centres.

Reflection:

Recall a moment when a particular sound or song transported you to another time or evoked a deep emotion. What memories and feelings surfaced?

____

____

____

____

The Resonance of Frequencies

Different frequencies affect us in unique ways. Lower frequencies, like the rhythm of drums, can ground us, connecting us to the Earth. Higher frequencies, such as the tingling of chimes, elevate our spirits, often aiding in transcending mundane concerns.

Harnessing these frequencies during meditation can amplify our introspective journeys. By aligning with specific sound frequencies, we can tap into various emotional and spiritual dimensions, bringing them to the forefront for exploration.

Activity:

Find a quiet space. Play a low-frequency sound, like drumbeats. Close your eyes, breathe deeply and let the sound envelop you. After a few minutes, switch to a high-frequency sound. Notice the shift in your inner landscape with each frequency.

Mantras and Chants: The Ancient Sonic Pathways

Since time immemorial, civilisations the world over have utilised the power of the spoken word for introspection and transformation. Mantras and chants aren't just words but vibrational frequencies that can reconfigure our internal energies. Whether it's the calming 'Om' in a yoga class or a heartfelt hymn in a church, vocalising our intentions and reflections can have a profound effect on our inner psyche.

When we give voice to our thoughts and intentions, it's as if we are amplifying our internal dialogue, allowing it to reverberate throughout our being. This practice isn't just about the sounds we produce but also about feeling their vibrations and the resulting resonance within us.

Repeating a mantra that is meaningful to you can help to bring clarity, focus and a profound inner peace. It is part and parcel of the meditative journey.

Mantras are not mere repetitions; they are sound energies that resonate with our very being. Chanting a mantra aligns our internal vibrations with universal frequencies, paving the way for a harmonious alignment within and with the universe.

Activity:

Choose a mantra that resonates with you. There are many different options in this space so find one that suits your needs. It could be a traditional one like the yoga "Om" or something personal such as an affirmation. Or you may want to explore Kirtan Kriya which is a timed finger movement and chant. Try to dedicate 15 minutes daily to this and observe the shifts within. The tranquillity and clarity this yields, even in stressful times, enables people to feel calmer and clearer with regular practice.

Nature's Symphony: A Deep Dive into Authenticity

Nature is the original composer. The chorus of crickets at dusk, the morning serenade of birds, the whisper of winds or the sounds of a babbling stream – these are all compositions that awaken our primal consciousness, connecting us with the authentic, raw essence of our being.

Nature has been serenading us since the beginning of time. Before the humdrum of urban life, our ancestors woke up to the sound of birds, bathed in babbling brooks and streams and danced to the sound of the wind. These sounds weren't mere background noise. They were, in essence, nature's music and a form of meditative guidance.

Activity:

Dedicate a weekend to nature. Find a tranquil spot—a forest, a serene beach, or even a quiet park in your city. Sit there with your eyes closed. Let nature's orchestra guide you into introspection. As you listen, note your feelings and revelations. It's astounding how many insights you'll gain from this simple yet profound exercise.

Submerging ourselves in nature's soundscape, devoid of modern life's cacophony, can offer deep introspective insights, reminding us of who we truly are beneath the everyday layers we wear.

Reflection:

Think of a time you were immersed in nature. It could be a forest, a beach, a river or lake. How did its soundscape affect you? Did it evoke a sense of connection, nostalgia or perhaps a deep-rooted peace?

____

____

____

____

____

Tuning into Inner Silence

Ironically, the most profound sound of all is silence. In silence, we can hear the unspoken, feel the intangible and connect with the infinite. It's the canvas on which the masterpiece of our introspection is painted. It can be especially beneficial in today's noisy world. Rare is the time when you can actually hear total silence.

Activity:

Dedicate a few minutes daily to bask in absolute silence. No music, no guided meditation, just silence. Observe the thoughts, memories and emotions that arise while you breathe deeply. Over time, you'll find this silence to be a powerful ally in your journey of self-awareness and inner peace.

Reflection:

Once you have tried this a few times, write down how it makes you feel. Has it become easier? Is it difficult or frustrating? Or have you found solace in your silence and achieved greater peace? Importantly, note that meditation, especially silent meditation, takes practice and can take a long time to master.

____

____

____

____

____

Sound, in its multitude of forms, is a potent tool for introspection. When used with intent, it can open doors within us, illuminating shadows, unveiling hidden feelings and nurturing growth. In the symphony of life, may you always find your unique note, resonating with authenticity, purpose and deep self-awareness.

"Listen to life, for it's playing your song."

The Magic of Sound in Meditation

Meditation is an age-old practice focused on centering the mind and finding clarity amid chaos. When sound is integrated into meditation, aside from chanting, it can elevate the experience, acting as an anchor that keeps the practitioner grounded, while allowing their consciousness to expand and explore.

Consider the gentle, consistent tolling of a meditation chime or bell such as the Tibetan bowl. Its sound not only signals the start or end of a practice but during meditation, it serves as a comforting reminder to return us to the present whenever the mind begins to wander.

Activity:

Get a Tibetan singing bowl or a simple bell. As you ring it, focus on the lingering resonance. Feel it coursing through your body, vibrating each cell. What memories or feelings does it evoke? Is there an inner turmoil it stirs? Or a profound peace that it instils? Document your journey with these sounds. They often act as doorways to long-forgotten memories or suppressed emotions.

____

____

____

____

____

The Power of Frequency: How Sound Affects Our Brain

Everything in the universe vibrates at a certain frequency, including our minds and bodies. Sound waves, particularly those used in meditative practices, align closely with the frequencies that resonate with our body and mind. This alignment can produce a deep sense of peace, clarity and balance.

Binaural beats, a modern discovery rooted in ancient practices, involve playing two slightly different frequencies in each ear. The brain perceives a third tone from these frequencies, guiding the brain from a state of alertness to one of deep meditation.

Nature's ambient sounds can be the bridge that helps us cross over this barrier, moving from a place of anxiety to a space of peace.

The Universal Language: Music

Music is an ethereal bridge connecting hearts and souls. Often, a musical piece can encapsulate emotions and memories, evoking feelings that words alone cannot express. For many, music is an indispensable tool for introspection, reflection and emotional release.

There's a reason why certain tracks or tunes resonate with us on a deeply personal level. It's because they mirror our internal rhythms, moods and sentiments. Diving deep into these melodies, we can explore uncharted territories of our mind and soul.

Digital Age Meditations: Guided Soundscapes

The digital age, for all its distractions, has also brought forth tools that can assist us in our introspective journeys. Guided meditations, binaural beats and soundscapes can act as modern-day conduits for achieving traditional meditative states.

Activity:

Explore platforms like YouTube or meditation apps that offer these auditory tools. Set aside a quiet hour or as much time as your schedule will allow you. Wear your headphones and let these digital soundscapes guide your thoughts. The juxtaposition of modern technology and ancient introspective practices can offer a uniquely enriching experience.

Concluding Thoughts

In the evolving chaos of modern life, sound serves as a timeless partner, guiding and accompanying us on our journey within. As we attune ourselves to the melodies and rhythms that surround us, we not only enhance our meditative practices but also deepen our understanding of the self.

Incorporating sound into our contemplative journeys might seem like a small shift, but its effects can be transformative.

As Jack Canfield beautifully encapsulates the spirit of personal growth:

"You only have control over three things in your life – the thoughts you think, the images you visualise, and the actions you take."

Sound, in all its forms, can also be an added potent tool to steer all three towards peace, understanding and enlightenment.

6

Archetypal Journeys: Identifying the Characters Within

Deep within the confines of our soul, nestled between layers of experience and memory, lie archetypes. These universally recognisable figures transcend time, culture and geography. They're not mere characters in stories; they're echoes of our very essence, both as individuals and as part of the collective unconscious.

In the tapestry of human experience, certain patterns are woven so deeply and consistently that they have solidified into these archetypal forms. Recognising and understanding these archetypes isn't just a study of ancient myths or a deep dive into literature. It's a personal journey, a mirror reflecting back the multifaceted nature of our inner world.

Stemming from the ancient Greek words "arché" (meaning beginning or original) and "typos" (meaning pattern or model), archetypes represent universally understood symbols and themes. They transcend cultural boundaries, acting as shared psychic experiences embedded in our collective unconscious.

As Jack Canfield once wisely remarked,

"In the vast expanse of human history and culture, despite our varied narratives, there's a surprising constancy – recurring

symbols and stories that cut across time, bridging ancient tribes to modern civilizations."

This constancy, these shared symbols, are what Carl Jung called archetypes.

1. The Hero: Stepping Out of the Ordinary

Symbolism: Every individual, at some point in their life, plays the role of the hero. It's the moment when they step out of their comfort zone, face challenges head-on and undergo transformation.

Anecdote: Despite facing significant setbacks in life, Lisa never gave up. Her hero's journey was one of transformation, overcoming challenges to become a beacon of hope both within and for her community.

Reflection: Recall a moment in your life when you felt called to challenge yourself. It might have been a physical journey or an emotional one. Did you heed that call? What potential obstacles did you face and how did they affect you?

Application: To channel the hero within, push your boundaries. Take on a new challenge, learn a new skill or confront a fear. The rewards will give you a great sense of achievement and contentment. Remember, the hero reminds us that challenges are but steppingstones, urging us to rise above, to evolve and to transform.

____

____

____

____

____

1.a The Hero and the Anti-Hero:

Symbolism: The hero, representing courage, determination and a willingness to sacrifice for the greater good, is a figure many aspire to be like. The anti-hero, on the other hand, embodies complex characteristics, often battling internal demons, yet possesses qualities we might reluctantly admire.

Anecdote: Lily, a dedicated firefighter, was always first on the scene, helping people and saving lives. She was the embodiment of a hero in her community. But off-duty, she battled addiction, mirroring the anti-hero. Understanding both these aspects of her personality, Lily sought help, not just for her addiction but to understand the root cause of her compulsions. This journey of introspection led her to find balance and peace.

2. The Shadow: Confronting the Darker Self

Symbolism: The shadow archetype represents the parts of ourselves we deny or suppress. It's our hidden desires, our unacknowledged fears and also our unrevealed potential.

Reflection: Think of a trait you dislike in others. Often, this can be a reflection of a suppressed part of our own psyche that we don't want to acknowledge. By recognising it we can achieve a greater sense of wholeness and acceptance.

Application: Set aside judgement and practice self-reflection. Understand that by embracing our shadows, we become more complete.

____

____

____

____

____

3. The Mentor: Guiding Light in Our Journey

Embodying the Spirit: Throughout our lives, we often find individuals who guide, nurture and provide wisdom. They help us navigate the tumultuous waters of life, offering insights borne from their own experience.

Reflection: Who has been a mentor in your life? What lessons did they impart that still resonate with you?

Application: Consider ways to share the wisdom you've accumulated. You might not see yourself as a mentor, but to someone else, you very well could be.

____

____

____

____

____

4. The Child: Innocence and Rediscovery

Symbolism: The child within us represents wonder, hope and a fresh perspective. Even in adulthood, this archetype emerges during moments of pure joy and unbridled curiosity.

Anecdote: David recalls a time when, during a challenging phase at work, he decided to take a day off and visit the local park. Sitting there, watching children play without a care in the world, he was reminded of the simple joys of life. The laughter, the spontaneity, the raw curiosity. That day, he decided to approach his challenges with the heart of a child – with enthusiasm, curiosity and without preconceived judgments. The results were astounding.

Reflection: When was the last time you saw the world through the eyes of wonder like children do? How can you cultivate this perspective in your daily life?

Application: Engage in childlike activities. Spend a day without plans, let curiosity guide you, or simply play without purpose. If you have children or grandchildren spend some time playing with them and lose yourself in their innocence, playfulness and joy.

____

____

____

____

____

5. The Maiden and The Warrior: Yin and Yang of the Soul

Embodying the Spirit: Every soul, regardless of gender or culture, carries the duality of the maiden's tenderness and the warrior's strength. It's the soft whisper that urges compassion and the assertive voice that champions boundaries.

Anecdote: Samantha grew up believing that showing vulnerability was a sign of weakness. Embodying the warrior's spirit, she powered through challenges without allowing herself a moment's rest. It wasn't until her own child reached out to her in a moment of vulnerability that Samantha realised the strength in softness and the power of the maiden's touch.

Reflection: Think about instances where you felt nurturing, or perhaps, protective. How did these moments make you feel about yourself? And also, a time when you felt strong and assertive? Are you comfortable with both energies or do you tend to suppress one over the other?

Application: Aim for balance. Neither the gentle grace of the maiden nor the determined strength of the warrior should overpower the other. Recognise situations where each energy would be beneficial. Balance is the goal.

____

____

____

____

____

6. The Trickster: Challenging Status Quo

Symbolism: Whilst in modern day this might be a term more used to describe a con artist or fraudster, the Trickster is an agent of change, the mischievous spirit pushing boundaries and questioning norms. This archetype reminds us that not everything is all it seems and sometimes, the established order needs a playful nudge. Perhaps in today's world that resonates with many more than ever.

Anecdote: During a company meeting, Jason, known for his playful attitude, posed an unexpected question that upended everyone's perspective. His "trickster" approach led to a revolutionary product idea.

Reflection: Was there a moment in your life where you questioned widely accepted norms? Did this lead to personal growth, transformation, or perhaps conversely a sense of isolation?

Application: Stay curious. Challenge beliefs, assumptions and perceptions. Let the trickster within guide you to innovative solutions and fresh perspectives. This is your inner being guiding you with your own truths.

____

____

____

____

7. The Sage: Pursuit of Wisdom

Embodying the Spirit: The sage seeks knowledge and, more importantly, understanding. This archetype resonates with introspection, reflection and a deep hunger for life's truths.

Reflection: What life experiences have gifted you with profound insights? How do you nurture your inner sage?

Application: Dedicate time for contemplation. Whether through meditation, journaling or simple silent reflection, let your inner wisdom surface.

____

____

____

____

____

8. The Outcast: Loneliness and Unique Perspective

Symbolism: Often misunderstood or side-lined, the outcast archetype embodies not only the pain of not belonging but also the unique insights that come from viewing things from the periphery.

Anecdote: Max always felt like the odd one out in school, his interests not aligning with his peers. Yet, this feeling of being an outcast allowed him to develop a unique perspective, leading him to become a renowned artist.

Reflection: Recall moments of feeling like an outsider. How did these moments shape your perspective? Did it make you feel isolated or did observance empower you and make you feel wise?

Application: Embrace your unique vantage point. While being an outcast can be painful, it also offers a distinctive lens to view the world and learn valuable life lessons without following the herd. The outcast sees the world from the periphery, providing insights that those at the centre might miss. Rather like the saying "can't see the wood for the trees."

____

____

____

____

____

8.a. The Hermit:

Symbolism: The hermit archetype signifies introspection, seeking answers within and soul searching. This is the journey inward, where solitude and reflection are tools for deeper understanding.

Anecdote: After a tragic accident, Sam withdrew from his social life. Friends worried as he spent days on end in isolation. But this period of solitude was transformative. He began to journal, meditate and engage in deep self-reflection. Through this hermit phase, Sam emerged more grounded and wrote a memoir that would go on to inspire millions about the strength of the human spirit and the need for inner reflection during challenging times.

Reflection: Can you recall a time when you withdrew, perhaps due to a painful experience? Did you learn from it and come out the other side equipped to continue or did you have to be coaxed by friends and family and struggle with it?

____

____

____

____

____

9. The Rebel: Breaking Chains and Defying Norms

Symbolism: The rebel is the spirit of revolution and defiance. They challenge the status quo, pushing boundaries and forging new paths, often leading to significant societal progress.

Anecdote: Maya, a senior executive at a traditional corporate firm, often felt the stifling nature of old-school bureaucracy. One day, she decided to trade her formal attire for more casual wear, representing her authentic self. It was a small act of defiance against the corporate culture. Her peers were initially taken aback, but soon a more relaxed dress code became the norm, leading to a more comfortable and authentic work environment.

Reflection: Can you recall a time when you felt empowered and liberated by directing another path not usually taken in any given situation? How good did it make you feel?

Application: By being true to your inner self and creating a difference beyond the norm in any circumstance can be extremely satisfying creating harmony and self-esteem within. Even little things can help you achieve this - it doesn't have to be a major act of defiance but even the smallest of challenges can have a great impact and lead to further self-progress.

____

____

____

____

____

11. The Ruler: Control, Power, and Responsibility

Symbolism: The ruler stands for authority, leadership and the societal structures that guide and protect us. They stand for governance, responsibility and the weight of decisions that come with power. The ruler often conjures images of absolute rule without compassion for the people they preside over but this is not usually the case.

Anecdote: Rahul, a community leader, found himself in the midst of a water crisis in his locality. While others were busy pointing fingers, he took the initiative to gather a team, source funds and establish a sustainable water purification system. His leadership not only resolved the crisis but brought the community closer together, proving that true leaders don't just command; they inspire action.

Reflection: Try to think of a time or a circumstance when you've gone above and beyond in leading and directing others the way to a positive outcome that was absent until you stepped in.

Application: Explore ways to lead others who will benefit from your ability to source the best outcome in a situation.

____

____

____

____

____

12. The Lover: Passion, Connection, and Intimacy

Symbolism: The lover embodies the deep emotional and spiritual connections we form with others. This archetype represents not just romantic passion but also the profound bonds of family, friendship and kinship.

Anecdote: Liam, who had always focused solely on his career, found himself attending a dance workshop during a vacation. There, he met Elise. Their connection was instant, transcending beyond physical attraction. They shared their stories, dreams and danced with such passion that went beyond their individual lifetime experiences. It was a reminder that love can be found in the most unexpected places and it's not always about romance but deep, soulful connection, hence the expression "soulmate."

Reflection: Most of us have a "love" that we cherish, whether it's a partner, spouse, children, other relatives or even pets. It's an enormously important part of our lives and our very souls and certain experiments in the past have demonstrated this. We simply cannot survive without love. It is the backbone of humanity.

Application: Take some quiet time to reflect on your "soulmate" or other deep love in your life and immerse yourself in appreciation of that love and how they have enriched your life and provided great comfort and joy.

____

____

____

____

____

13. The Caregiver: Compassion, Generosity and Selflessness

Symbolism: The caregiver embodies the purest forms of love and sacrifice. They signify the nurturing aspects of human nature, always putting others before themselves and embodying empathy in its truest sense.

Anecdote: Maria, a schoolteacher, once narrated an incident of a student who'd been particularly challenging throughout the year. Instead of reprimanding him, she chose one day to sit down and listen. She discovered layers she hadn't seen – challenges at home, bullying and immense pressure. By tapping into her caregiver archetype, she was able to build a bridge of understanding and transformed not just the student's academic year, but potentially the rest of his life.

Reflection: Have there been times in your life when you haven't taken the time to really listen to someone who you find challenging or disrupting? Could you have made a difference? Or, perhaps, you feel someone could have given you more space and attention to reach a better understanding and harmonious relationship in a certain circumstance or period of your life?

Application: Whilst you cannot change historical events and past relationship experiences, you can ponder on this and be mindful when you face a situation with someone you consider difficult and remember that giving them some more time and attention could enrich their experience and make for a better outcome all round.

____

____

____

____

Reflection from Jack's Journal

"Our personal myths are like an internal compass. They guide our steps, even when we are unaware. To become conscious of these motifs, these recurring patterns in the story of our life, is to gain a measure of control and purpose."

Reflection and Integration:

Archetypes are not just mere characters in tales; they reside within each of us. Recognizing them can illuminate our paths, helping us understand our actions, reactions, desires and fears. The dance between these archetypes, their battles, unions and transformations mirror our own life journey.

By reflecting on these archetypal patterns, we become more equipped to handle life's challenges, to understand the roles we play in different life stages and situations, and to harness the strengths each archetype offers.

It's important, however, not to pigeonhole ourselves into one archetype or another. We are fluid beings, constantly evolving. At different junctures of life and events, different archetypes might dominate our psyche. The key is to recognize their influence, learn from them and harness their energy in a way that aligns with our authentic selves.

Personal Exercise: Think of one stand out moment in your life where you've strongly embodied one of these archetypes. Write down the feelings, thoughts and actions associated with that period. Now, envision a scenario where another archetype might have been more beneficial. How would that have changed the outcome? This reflection is not about regret but understanding and growth.

____

____

____

____

____

Bringing Archetypes into Daily Life

Incorporating the understanding of these archetypes into our daily lives is about recognising patterns, both in our behaviour and in the stories we're drawn to. These patterns provide insights, helping us make sense of our reactions, choices and relationships.

For instance, if you find yourself constantly drawn to stories of brave knights and dangerous quests, perhaps your inner hero is urging for a challenge or a change. Or if tales of wise old wizards captivate you, maybe it's a call to deepen your knowledge or mentor someone else.

Exercise: Reflect on your favourite tales or movies. What patterns or archetypes do you see consistently appearing? How do they mirror your own life and aspirations?

____

____

____

____

____

By understanding these archetypes, we access deeper layers of our psyche, connecting with the universal tales woven into the fabric of humanity. They serve as guides, steering us towards greater self-awareness and a richer, more profound understanding of our place in the tapestry of existence.

7

DREAMSCAPES AND THE SUBCONSCIOUS - INTRODUCING THE MYSTIQUE AND REVELATIONS OF DREAMS.

As night envelopes the world in its inky embrace and our external senses mute, a different kind of path unfolds — a journey into the depths of our subconscious mind, often through vivid dreamscapes.

Dreams, a common yet deeply mystical phenomenon, have captivated human curiosity for aeons. These nightly escapades, though fleeting, leave lingering feelings — sometimes of joy, sometimes of confusion and occasionally a haunting fear or even terror.

The eminent Carl Jung once said,

"Who looks outside, dreams; who looks inside, awakes."

"The dream is a little hidden door in the innermost and most secret recesses of the soul."

The Mirror of the Soul

At the heart of our dream world lies a mirror, reflecting not our physical visage but the web of our emotions, experiences and, at times, even unspoken desires. Like a painter's canvas, dreams capture the essence of our life, painting abstracts that hold secrets awaiting interpretation.

Anecdote: Sarah often dreamt of flying. These dreams weren't spurred by a longing for flight but symbolised her deep-seated desire for freedom. It wasn't until she attended a workshop on dreams that she realised her soul's craving to break from life's monotony and make some serious changes.

The Revelations from the Abyss & their Meanings:

Dreams aren't merely a recreation of our daily lives. They're rife with symbolism, archetypes and motifs that, when understood, can offer profound insights. Some of them are pretty harmless whilst others can be more unsettling.

Recurring Dreams: If a dream or theme keeps recurring, it's usually a sign that there's an unresolved issue or a significant message the subconscious is trying to convey.

Anecdote: Jake, who consistently dreamt of missing a train, eventually identified that this was related to his fears of missing out – not just in his professional life but in personal relationships and experiences.

Common and Recurring Dreams:

- **The Pursuing Monster**: A common dream scenario, where one is being chased by something or somebody terrifying. This typically indicates evasion in waking life—perhaps avoiding a confrontation or a challenging situation.

- **Losing Teeth:** While unsettling, this common recurring dream is often thought to represent a lack of confidence or fear of helplessness and even ageing.

- **Flying:** Whether it's soaring above cities or fluttering like a butterfly in the breeze, flying dreams can signify a desire to escape or achieve greater freedom in one's life.

- **Falling:** This is another very common dream where people think they are falling into an abyss or off the edge of a cliff, for example. This can symbolise a sense of losing control and a feeling of helplessness in one's life.

- **Drowning or suffocating:** This is also a familiar dream pattern and can be very disturbing as it can create sleep apnoea and the dreamer can awake gasping for air. It often symbolises feelings of being totally overwhelmed and stressed and should be recognised as such and appropriate action taken to reduce pressure and anxiety.

- **Being Naked in Public:** This can be a sign of vulnerability, shame, embarrassment and general insecurity with oneself and, although uncomfortable, is also very commonplace.

Nightmares and Facing our Shadows:

As mentioned, not all dreams are pleasant or simply odd. Nightmares can be particularly disturbing. However, instead of dismissing them, they can be viewed as tools for introspection. They often spotlight our insecurities, traumas or repressed memories, asking us to face them head-on.

Anecdote: Liam had a recurring nightmare where he was trapped in a burning building. After engaging in deep introspection, he connected this with a traumatic childhood incident. Addressing it and seeking therapy transformed not just his dream pattern but his waking life.

By decoding these dreams, we are not only able to understand our fears and desires but also get a roadmap, albeit a cryptic one, guiding our journey to personal growth.

Decoding the Language of the Subconscious

Dreams speak in a unique language – a mix of symbolism, metaphors and sometimes even direct messages. Decoding this language requires patience and introspection.

Symbolism: Much like in literature or art, dreams often convey their meaning through symbols. A raging storm, for instance, could represent internal turmoil, while a broken bridge might symbolise a ruptured relationship or missed opportunity.

Anecdote: Sarah often dreamt of losing her shoes – sometimes leaving them behind at a party, at other times misplacing them at work. Upon reflection, she realised these dreams began after she made a career move she wasn't entirely confident about. For her, the shoes represented a grounding, a sense of belonging, and her dream highlighted her subconscious anxieties.

Engaging actively with our dreams, rather than dismissing them as mere oddities of the night, can be deeply transformative.

1. **Dream Journaling:** One of the most recommended practices is keeping a dream journal. Upon waking, before the tendrils of the dream slip away, jot down every detail

you are able to recall. Over time, you may see patterns emerge, offering certain insights into your psyche.

2. **Guided Imagery:** Once familiar with recurring dream symbols, employ guided imagery. For instance, if consistently encountering a locked door in dreams, visualise unlocking it. This conscious intervention can lead to breakthroughs in understanding blockages or suppressed feelings.

3. **Dream Sharing:** Sharing dreams with trusted individuals or groups can provide external perspectives, helping decipher complex motifs or symbols. Dream workshops can be especially helpful if you have access to one.

Dreams as Catalysts for Growth

Dreams, when approached with curiosity rather than scepticism, can be powerful tools for self-awareness and personal evolution. They invite introspection, nudging us to confront deep-seated fears, acknowledge suppressed desires and celebrate joys that we might overlook in waking life.

Anecdote: James, a highly pragmatic individual, had a recurring dream of a bird trapped in a cage. Over time, and with introspection, he began to recognise that this reflected his own stifling professional life. Harnessing the symbolism of this dream, James embarked on a journey of self-discovery, eventually transitioning to a career that resonated with his passions.

The Therapeutic Power of Dreams

Research has increasingly shown that dreams can play a therapeutic role in our lives. For those battling traumas or deeply entrenched fears, dreams can provide a safe space to confront and process these emotions. They serve as a nightly therapy session, allowing us to grapple with and often resolve issues subconsciously.

Anecdote: Lisa, a war veteran, frequently experienced night terrors. However, over time and with dedicated dream work, these nightmares transformed. The battlefields gave way to serene landscapes, signifying her inner journey of healing from the scars of war.

Lucid Dreaming: Active Participation in the Dream World

Lucid dreaming is the conscious awareness during a dream state. It's when the dreamer knows they're in a dream and can, to varying extents, control its outcome. This form of dreaming can be harnessed for personal growth, problem-solving and even overcoming personal barriers.

Anecdote: Anna, after months of practising lucid dreaming techniques, was able to confront a dream character representing her self-doubt. This confrontation, in the dreamscape, led to a significant boost in her real-world confidence.

The Path to Lucid Dreaming:

One of the most empowering aspects of dream work is lucid dreaming – the ability to become conscious within a dream and even direct its course. It's like becoming the director of your own nightly film, crafting narratives and outcomes.

1. **Reality Checks:** Throughout the day, periodically ask yourself, "Am I dreaming?" This awake practice heightens your awareness and seeps into your dream state, increasing the chances of a lucid dream.

2. **Mnemonic Induction:** As you drift to sleep, repeat, "I will know I'm dreaming." This affirmation enhances dream recall and lucidity which is highly useful if you are engaging in dreamwork.

3. **Wake Back to Bed:** Waking up after 5-6 hours of sleep and then drifting off again has shown increased chances

of lucidity, as this phase is rich in REM sleep where vivid dreams occur.

From Dreams to Reality

Beyond the therapeutic and the mystical, dreams hold the power to inspire. History is replete with tales of inventors, artists and philosophers who derived inspiration from their dreams.

Anecdote*: Paul McCartney of The Beatles once woke up with a tune in his head, which he quickly jotted down. This melody would later become the iconic song, "Yesterday." Such is the power of dreams – they transcend the boundaries of imagination and can usher in tangible creations in our waking world.

The Mystique of Nightly Sojourns

There's an undeniable magic in dreams. The very idea that our mind, unfettered by the confines of the day to day waking reality, weaves tales, crafts scenarios and constructs worlds and is a testament to human creativity and depth. These dreamscapes serve as reminders that beneath the veneer of daily routines and pragmatism lies a universe brimming with possibilities, waiting to be explored.

For anyone on a path to self-awareness and growth, dreams offer a treasure trove of wisdom. They are not just the random firing of neurons but a dance of the subconscious, filled with clues, lessons and revelations.

As we lay down each night, ready to embark on another dreamy adventure, let's do so with an open heart and an inquisitive mind. For in the theatre of dreams, every scene, character and nuance hold the potential to illuminate our path, guiding us closer to our true selves and where we want to be.

Concluding Thoughts: Embracing the Night

Dreams have fascinated humans for millennia. They serve as a mirror to our deepest fears, desires, regrets and aspirations. While our modern, fast-paced world often relegates dreams to the fringes of importance, recognising and embracing their profound impact can be both cathartic and transformative. Dreams are the unsung bridge between our conscious and subconscious minds, between our known selves and the vast reservoir of our uncharted psyche.

To truly grow, to journey towards self-awareness, embracing our dreams plays a significant role. Dreams challenge us, comfort us, sometimes frighten us, perplex us and often guide us. As we stand at the threshold of sleep each night, let's remember that we are about to enter a realm of infinite possibilities, where every dream is a step towards understanding our deeper selves.

In the wise words of Edgar Cayce...

"Dreams are today's answers to tomorrow's questions." So, let's dream with purpose, introspect with intent, and evolve with every revelation our subconscious graciously bestows upon us."

In the words of Edgar Allan Poe,

"Those who dream by day are cognizant of many things which escape those who dream only by night."

Embrace your dreams, for they are the silent messengers of your subconscious, guiding you towards a more awakened, authentic life.

8

Emotional Ecosystems
- A detailed exploration of emotions and their interrelations.

Introduction:

The Rich Tapestry of Our Inner World

Every individual, at their core, is a vibrant and complex tapestry woven from countless threads of emotion. These threads, with their varied hues and textures, shape our experiences, decisions and interactions with others. They are not isolated strands but are intricately interconnected, creating an ecosystem within us as complex and dynamic as any found in nature.

In this exploration, we'll journey into the heart of this ecosystem, aiming to understand the profound interrelations between our emotions and ultimately to navigate them with grace and purpose.

1. Mapping the Emotional Landscape

To understand our emotional ecosystem, we must first recognize its vastness. Emotions are not merely feelings; they are signals, informing us about our internal state in relation to our external environment. Joy, sorrow, anger, jealousy, curiosity – these are but landmarks in an extensive emotional geography.

Joy may be likened to a sunlit meadow, where we feel warmth, light and expansiveness. In contrast, *sorrow* can be envisioned as a deep canyon where shadows linger, but where the echoes can lead to profound insights.

But what about those emotions we struggle to name? Those subtle blends of feelings that don't quite fit into conventional categories? These are the hidden groves and secret waterfalls of our inner world, waiting to be discovered and understood.

2. Emotions in Interplay: The Dance of Experience

It's a rare moment when we feel a singular, unblended emotion. More often, our feelings are intricate medleys of experience, where multiple emotions twirl and intertwine.

Much like colours on a canvas, emotions are seldom experienced in isolation. Often, they blend, mix and interact, creating a rich blend of experiences.

Fear can coexist with excitement; sadness can intertwine with hope and anger might walk hand in hand with love. Such is the complexity of our emotional world.

Consider nostalgia – a blend of joy and sorrow. It's the joy of cherished memories and the sorrow of times long gone.

Or take the sensation of a "bittersweet" moment, where happiness and sadness coexist, making the experience all the more poignant.

But beyond these named blends, countless unnamed emotional combinations ebb and flow within us daily. Recognizing this dance, this interplay, is crucial. It reminds us that emotions are not static; they evolve, influenced by each other and our experiences.

3. Emotions as Catalysts: Harnessing Energy for Growth

Emotions, powerful as they are, have the potential to propel significant personal growth. They are not mere experiences to be felt, forgotten and put aside but are reservoirs of energy waiting to be harnessed.

For instance, anger, often viewed negatively, can be a driving force for change if channelled correctly. It can ignite passion and spur actions that reshape our lives, on a personal and societal level. Similarly, periods of introspection and melancholy can lead to the most profound personal revelations and creative outputs.

The key lies in understanding, not judging or suppressing. When we approach our emotions as allies, as guides, we unlock a transformative power within.

4. Navigating the Emotional Ecosystem: Tools for the Journey

To journey through this emotional landscape with purpose and clarity, we need tools. Introspection is our compass, helping us recognise where we currently stand. Empathy is our bridge, allowing us to connect with and understand others' emotional terrains. And mindfulness is our anchor, ensuring we remain present, even amidst the fiercest emotional storms.

Engaging with our emotions is not a passive act. It requires effort, patience and often, courage. But as with any journey, the rewards are worth the challenges. For in understanding our emotional ecosystems, we not only come to understand ourselves better but also the world around us.

5. The Layers of Emotional Depth: Beyond the Surface

If we liken our emotions to an ocean, then what we often perceive on the surface is merely a fraction of its entirety. Beneath the surface waves of immediate reactions lie the deeper currents of long-held feelings, shaped by memories, experiences and even ancestral narratives.

Take, for example, an unexpected surge of anger at a minor inconvenience. On the surface, it might seem disproportionate. But diving deeper, it might reveal a reservoir of unaddressed frustrations, perhaps stemming from feelings of powerlessness in childhood.

By venturing below the surface, we begin to understand the origins of our emotions, allowing us to address the root causes rather than just the manifestations.

6. Emotional Feedback: The Mirroring World

Our external environment often mirrors our internal emotional state. When we're joyful, the world seems brighter, more vibrant. Conversely, during our melancholic phases, it can appear dull, almost monochromatic.

This mirroring isn't merely perceptual. Our emotions can influence our actions and decisions, shaping our realities. A person driven by optimism might take risks, leading to new opportunities, while someone bound by fear might remain in their comfort zone, limiting their growth.

Recognizing this feedback loop between our inner emotions and outer world can empower us to make conscious choices, aligning our external realities with our desired emotional states.

7. The Ripple Effect: Emotions in a Shared Space

Emotions aren't solitary and static. They resonate, creating ripples that touch those around us. A simple smile can lift someone's day, while a harsh word might cast shadows on another's spirit.

In this interconnected web of human interactions, our emotional states play a significant role. They influence group dynamics, impact collective decision-making, and shape shared narratives.

Consider the contagious nature of laughter. One person's genuine laughter can ignite a chain reaction, elevating the mood of an entire group. Conversely, shared grief can create strong bonds of empathy and understanding, uniting individuals in mutual support.

By recognizing our role in this shared emotional space, we learn the importance of emotional responsibility, ensuring that our ripples create waves of positivity rather than being destructive or hurtful.

8. Emotional Alchemy: Transmuting Emotions for Growth

All emotions, including the ones perceived as negative, carry potential energy for growth. The process of transmuting these emotions, converting them from raw, often overwhelming sensations into constructive forces, is akin to alchemy.

For instance, channelling the restless energy of anxiety into creative pursuits can lead to artistic masterpieces. Similarly, the deep introspection during periods of sadness can birth profound insights and wisdom.

Emotional alchemy requires awareness, intention and practice. It's an art, refining our feelings, distilling them and harnessing their essence for our betterment.

9. Emotions as Guides: Tuning into Internal Compasses

Every emotion, no matter how fleeting or profound, carries a message. When we feel joy, it's a sign that we're aligned with our desires and values. Contrarily, recurring frustration might indicate misalignment with our environment or a need to establish boundaries.

By tuning into these emotional cues, we transform them into guides. Instead of drowning in the tidal waves of overwhelm, we can surf them, navigating our journey with discernment and wisdom.

Take a moment to reflect on a recent emotion that felt particularly intense. What might it be signalling? Perhaps it's a nudge towards a change, a reassurance of being on the right path or a call for introspection?

10. Emotional Resilience: Cultivating Flexibility

Emotional resilience is the art and skill of bouncing back from adversities, harnessing challenges as springboards for growth. It doesn't mean suppressing or ignoring emotions but rather navigating them with grace, perspective and adaptive strategies.

To cultivate resilience, one needs to practise flexibility in emotional responses, reframing challenges, nurturing a positive outlook and fostering connections. Remember, resilience is not a trait we're born with but a muscle we build over time. Every challenge, every setback and every tear shed is an opportunity to strengthen this muscle, preparing us for future storms and sunnier days alike.

11. The Call for Emotional Intelligence: Beyond IQ

In a rapidly evolving world, emotional intelligence (EQ) has gained prominence in more recent times, often overshadowing traditional intelligence (IQ). EQ encompasses self-awareness, self-regulation, motivation, empathy and social skills. It's the ability to recognise, understand and manage our emotions while also tuning into and influencing the emotions of others.

A high EQ can lead to better relationships, career success and overall well-being. By nurturing our EQ, we not only enrich our individual lives but also contribute positively to our communities, building bridges of understanding, compassion and collaboration.

Conclusion:

Emotions are the heartbeat of our existence, pulsating rhythms of joy, sorrow, fear, excitement and myriad shades in between. By diving deep into our emotional ecosystems, we not only gain insights into our authentic selves but also evolve as more empathetic, resilient and emotionally intelligent beings. Such is the beauty and power of understanding the interrelations of our emotions.

9

Art of Visualisation: Empowering the Imagination as a Tool for Self-Discovery

***Introductory Musings*:**

In a world overfilled with external stimuli, it's easy to forget the vast landscapes that reside within us, waiting to be explored. Visualisation is more than just a mental exercise; it's a bridge between the tangible and the intangible, an oasis of creativity and a haven for the spirit.

Consider for a moment the great inventors, visionaries and dreamers throughout history. Whether it was Nikola Tesla envisioning his inventions in intricate detail before they were physically manifested or Walt Disney dreaming of magical kingdoms, the power of visualisation has long been a conduit for transformation.

1. The Science Behind Visualization: Brain Meets Imagination

Recent studies in neuroscience have unveiled the wonders of our brain's capacity when engaged in visualisation. Neuroplasticity, the ability of the brain to change and adapt, comes alive when we visualise. By imagining scenarios, actions or tasks, we activate many of the same brain regions that light up during actual physical execution.

It has been scientifically proven that the brain cannot distinguish between a strong thought or visualisation and external reality. Therefore, if you practise visualisation for specific goals or desires, it will bring you closer to achieving them.

For instance, athletes often employ visualisation techniques to enhance performance, tapping into the brain's ability to recreate and perfect motions, even if just performed in the mind's eye. This mental rehearsal strengthens neural pathways, making the actual execution more precise.

Exercise: Mental Rehearsal

1. Find a quiet space and sit comfortably.

2. Close your eyes and take a few deep breaths.

3. Visualise a task you wish to perfect (e.g., a dance move, a presentation).

4. Run through the action in meticulous detail in your mind, feeling every movement and emotion.

5. Repeat multiple times, refining and enhancing with each iteration.

2. Visualisation as a Portal to Self-Discovery

Visualisation isn't solely a tool for enhancing skills; it's also a pathway to understanding oneself more deeply. By visualising our aspirations, desires and even fears, we can uncover hidden facets of our psyche.

For instance, if you visualise your ideal day or your perfect environment, the elements that surface can offer insights into what truly resonates with your soul. The colours, the settings, the people you imagine—all these components can shed light on your core desires and values.

Exercise: Journey to Your Ideal Self

1. Find a serene spot and take a few calming breaths.

2. Picture yourself in a scene where you feel genuinely content and fulfilled.

3. Notice the details: Where are you? Who is with you? What activities are you engaged in?

4. As the scene unfolds, pay attention to emotions that arise.

5. Once completed, jot down your observations and reflect on what these insights reveal about your true self.

---

3. Harnessing Imagination for Healing and Growth

Visualisation can also be a saviour for the soul, aiding in healing past traumas and moulding a brighter future. By visualising scenarios where we confront our fears or past pains and emerge victorious, we can reshape our internal narratives. Over time, these positive visual narratives can alter our beliefs and self-perception.

Moreover, the act of visualisation stimulates the release of serotonin, a neurotransmitter linked to happiness and well-being. By immersing ourselves in positive mental imagery, we inadvertently boost our mood and resilience.

Exercise: Embracing Healing Imagery

1. Settle into a relaxed state, ensuring minimal disturbances.

2. Envision a sanctuary—a place where you feel safe and loved.

3. In this sanctuary, imagine confronting a past hurt or fear. Instead of succumbing, visualise yourself being supported, understood and ultimately triumphant.

4. Bask in the positive emotions, allowing them to wash over you, cleansing past wounds.

5. Return from the visualisation, holding onto the strength and positivity you've garnered.

4. Crafting Your Future through Visualization

Every great achievement begins with a vision. By visualising our goals in vivid detail, we not only set a clear direction but also muster the motivation to achieve them. Each time you mentally 'live' your dreams, you reinforce your commitment and stoke the fires of passion making them more likely to become a reality.

Exercise: Building Tomorrow Today

1. Begin by relaxing your body and mind.

2. Now, picture a milestone you wish to achieve in the future.

3. Experience it in full sensory detail: the emotions, the surroundings, the accolades.

4. Allow the joy and pride of the accomplishment to permeate your being.

5. The Emotional Alchemy: Transmuting Pain into Purpose

The beauty of human existence is its kaleidoscope of emotions; however, within this vast spectrum, there are moments of pain and anguish. Rather than dreading these challenging times, we can see them as opportunities for growth and transformation. By viewing our emotional experiences as a form of alchemy, we can turn base emotions into golden insights.

Recognizing Emotional Gold

In every emotional challenge lies an opportunity. The raw materials—whether it's heartbreak, disappointment or fear—hold the potential to be transmuted into a greater understanding of oneself.

Anecdote: Sarah was always afraid of public speaking. However, when her best friend was unable to deliver a speech due to sudden illness, Sarah was thrust into the spotlight. Instead of shying away, she confronted her fear. While her voice wavered initially, she soon found her rhythm and by the end of the speech, not only had she overcome her fear but discovered a passion for public speaking.

The Process of Transmutation

This is more than mere positive thinking; it's about deep internal work. It requires:

1. **Acknowledgment:** Recognizing and accepting the emotion without judgement.

2. **Understanding:** Digging deeper into why this emotion arose. What triggered it? Are there past experiences that are linked to it?

3. **Reframing:** Looking at the situation from a fresh perspective. What can be learned from this? How can this challenge become an opportunity?

4. **Action:** Taking proactive steps, either by changing one's mindset, seeking help, or directly addressing the root cause.

Anecdote: Jason, after a series of failed ventures, was overwhelmed by feelings of inadequacy. Instead of giving up, he sought mentorship. Through this guidance, he learned to view his failures not as evidence of inadequacy, but as steppingstones and lessons to achieve his goals. His next venture was a roaring success.

Creating Your Philosopher's Stone

In alchemy, the Philosopher's Stone is a legendary substance said to be capable of turning base metals into gold. In our emotional alchemy, the Philosopher's Stone represents our individual processes, tools and mindsets that enable emotional transmutation.

Anecdote: Mia, grappling with the grief of losing her mother, began journaling. This act, simple yet profound, became her Philosopher's Stone. Through writing, she processed her grief, celebrated her mother's memories and gradually found a way to move forward in peace and gratitude.

Cultivating Resilience and Growth

The final step in emotional alchemy is about cultivating resilience. It's about recognising that life will invariably present challenges, but with our Philosopher's Stone at hand, we can face them head-on.

Anecdote: When Aiden's relationship ended, he was devastated. However, remembering past challenges and the tools he'd developed, he approached this heartbreak with resilience. He gave himself time to heal, leaned on his support system and emerged stronger, wiser and more open-hearted.

In embracing the art of emotional alchemy, we're not just navigating life's challenges; we're actively shaping our journey, turning every setback into a setup for a comeback, and every pain into a steppingstone towards joy and fulfilment.

6. The Architect's Blueprint: Structuring Your Visions

The visual realm of our psyche isn't merely a fantastical playground. It's also the drawing board where our future takes shape. Like a master architect reviewing blueprints, our ability to visualise, refine and reconstruct our goals and ambitions lends substance to our dreams.

Imagine for a moment you're standing before a vast open plot of land, your toolbelt secured and blueprints in hand. This plot represents your life. What structures will you build here? What kind of terrain will you sculpt? The choices are endless, and they're all yours.

Visualisation is not just about seeing with the mind's eye; it's about shaping and designing, much like an architect does. Every detail counts – from the foundational ideas to the ornate embellishments.

Anecdote: Sarah always wanted to write a book, but the mere thought overwhelmed her. But instead of seeing it as a monumental task, she began visualising every chapter as a room in a house. She visualised herself designing each room, deciding its theme, its contents, its ambience. This restructuring not only made the process enjoyable but also organised. Soon enough, her mental house translated to a published book.

7. Future-Casting: Directing the Course of Destiny

The visualisation process isn't constrained to the present; it can be a dynamic bridge to the future. By painting clear and hopeful pictures of what is yet to come, we empower ourselves to take steps that align with those visions.

Picture this: A boat in the vast ocean, not merely drifting, but being directed by a clear path of luminescent markers leading the way.

By visualising our futures in a vivid, positive light, we're setting these luminescent markers for ourselves. The clearer our visions, the clearer our path.

Anecdote: Jake was at a low point in his life, unsure of his next steps. He began a practice of visualising himself in a serene, successful future scenario every night. Over time, this imagery became so palpable that he started recognising opportunities in his daily life that seemed to resonate with this future vision. It's as if he'd created a map and the universe began showing him the way.

8. Visionary Puzzles: Interlocking Dreams with Reality

Every dream can be broken down into pieces, rather like a jigsaw puzzle. These pieces are the steps, the milestones and the actions needed. Visualising our goals as interconnected puzzles can make daunting aspirations more manageable and achievable.

Think of your biggest aspiration. Now, picture it as a 1000-piece jigsaw puzzle. Each piece, no matter how small, is crucial to the final picture.

The act of visualisation assists us in understanding which pieces of our dreams and goals fit together, giving us a clearer understanding of the path to our goals.

Anecdote: Riya dreamt of opening her own art gallery. The sheer magnitude of this task often left her paralysed with doubt. However, she started breaking this massive goal into smaller, visualisable pieces. First finding a venue, then connecting with artists and onto planning the launch event - each was a piece of her dream puzzle. As she meticulously assembled each part, her dream gallery finally came to life.

9. Dynamic Landscapes: Adapting and Evolving Visions

Life is never static, and our visions shouldn't be either. As we grow, learn and evolve, so should the images we create in our minds. Holding onto outdated or restrictive visions can limit our potential.

Imagine a landscape painting that morphs with time, incorporating new elements, adapting to seasons and evolving to become richer and more diverse.

That's how our visualisations should be – alive, dynamic and ever-responsive to our growth.

Anecdote: Leonard had always visualised himself as a corporate honcho. But midway through his career, he discovered his passion for teaching. Instead of sticking to his old visions, he let them evolve. He visualised classrooms, engaging lectures and inspired students. Over time, he became a respected professor, living a life more fulfilling than he'd ever thought possible prior to the visualisation techniques he'd employed.

Conclusion:

Visualisation is more than a technique; it's an art form that enables us to connect deeply with our innermost desires, hopes and dreams. Through its practice, we don't just see; we create, evolve and manifest. It's a testament to the power of the human spirit, our brains and our boundless imagination.

10

Blank Canvas Sections: Let Your Soul Speak

"In every human being there is a special heaven whole and unbroken." - Paracelsus

Every journey into the depths of the soul brings about a whirlwind of emotions, insights and revelations. There will be moments of clarity that strike like lightning and emotions that flow like a gentle stream, evading definition or structure. It's in these moments that our subconscious most ardently wishes to communicate.

This is why the Blank Canvas Sections are integral to your journey. They're spaces without structure, without guiding questions or tasks, allowing the raw, unfiltered language of your soul to flourish.

How to Utilise the Blank Canvas Sections:

- **Unrestrained Flow:** When an insight, emotion, lightbulb idea or realisation strikes, don't wait! Grab a pen and start scribbling. These moments of intense clarity or emotion are fleeting. Capture them.

- **Artistic Revelations:** Sometimes, words fall short. Maybe your revelations come as symbols, images or abstract drawings. Let the ink or pencil flow in tune with your intuition.

- **Embrace the Silence:** It's okay if some blank sections remain untouched. They might resonate with moments of stillness, signifying peace, contemplation or simply being.

- **Memorabilia of Moments:** Maybe it's a leaf from the garden where you had a profound realisation, or a ticket stub from the cinema where a film resonated with a personal experience. Place them here. This is your canvas of memories, after all.

Inspirational Quotes to Kindle Your Flame:

- **"The soul becomes dyed with the colour of its thoughts."** - Marcus Aurelius

- **"Words are a pretext. It is the inner bond that draws one person to another, not words."** - Rumi

- **"The unexamined life is not worth living."** - Socrates

- **"One can have no smaller or greater mastery than mastery of oneself."** - Leonardo da Vinci

- **"Your visions will become clear only when you can look into your own heart. Who looks outside, dreams; who looks inside, awakes."** - Carl Jung

- **Whether you think you can or think you can't, either way you are right"** - Henry Ford

By giving voice to your internal journey, whether through words, sketches or mementos, you're not just documenting; you're honouring your path and your inner being. Let this section be a testament to the diversity and beauty of your introspective odyssey.

11

Conclusion and Further Resources: Lighting the Path Ahead

The voyage within is as vast and infinite as the cosmos itself. It is a journey that transcends the physical, venturing deep into the uncharted territories of our minds and our very essence. Through the pages of this journal, you have embarked on an odyssey of inner exploration, facing shadows, embracing revelations and illuminating the corners of your being previously obscured by shadow.

Your Odyssey So Far:

Remember that introspection, like any profound journey, does not end; it only evolves. Every step you took, every prompt you pondered upon and every canvas you filled is not an end in itself but a marker for the next leg of your journey.

With every shadow you confronted, you unveiled a part of your story. With every doodle, sketch or poetic line, you gave voice to your inner symphonies. By committing to this profound process, you've taken brave strides towards holistic growth and self-awareness.

The Path Ahead:

It's essential to remember that personal growth is not linear. There might be days of profound insight followed by moments of stillness. Embrace each phase. The stillness is as revealing as the storm. It is in the quiet moments that the seeds of understanding take root, preparing to blossom when the time is right.

Further Resources for Your Journey:

For those hungry for more, the quest for self-understanding never ceases. Here are some handpicked resources that can guide you further:

Books:

- *"The Undiscovered Self"* by Carl Jung - A Dive into the Depths of the Subconscious.

- *"The Book of Awakening"* by Mark Nepo - Daily Meditations for a More Conscious Living.

- *"Man's Search for Meaning"* by Viktor E. Frankl - A Journey of Finding Purpose in Life's Most Challenging Moments.

- *"The Power of Now"* by Eckhart Tolle - A Guide to Spiritual Enlightenment

- *"The Secret"* by Rhonda Byrne

- *"Chicken Soup for the Soul"* by Jack Canfield and Mark Victor Hansen

- *"15 Minutes to Destiny: The Proven Blueprint to Transform Your Life Instantly"* by Ellie & James Richards

And for Fun...

- *"Titans of Thought"* by Ellie and James Richards - Brain Quest with Puzzles, Trivia and Insights from 50 Global Visionaries

Online Platforms:

- Insight Timer: A vast collection of guided meditations and teachings from world-renowned experts.

  - Inner Journey Workshops: Virtual workshops focusing on deepening self-awareness and growth available on select online platforms.

Retreats and Workshops:

- Mindful Me Retreats: Weekend retreats focusing on introspection, yoga, alternative therapies and holistic wellbeing.

- The Self-Discovery Workshop Series: Monthly workshops exploring different facets of the human psyche.

Community Groups:

This is another great way to connect with likeminded people on a regular basis to continue your path of growth and enlightenment.

Please note that these are just a handful of suggestions and we would encourage further research on your part since geographical location will be relevant when seeking workshops and retreats.

In the grand tapestry of life, every thread, be it light or shadow, has its purpose. As you step forth from this diary, carry with you the wisdom of your experiences and the hunger for further discovery. Your journey within is a lifelong adventure, one that constantly offers new horizons, deeper understandings and infinite possibilities.

Embrace it with open arms and an open heart!

Thank you!

A Heartfelt Note to Our Readers,

As I pen down this message, I am overwhelmed with gratitude. Your journey through these pages is not just a testament to your commitment towards personal growth, but also a reflection of the shared human experience that binds us all. Every word in this book was crafted with deep love and a genuine wish to illuminate pathways toward self-awareness and personal evolution.

Love and compassion are often lacking in today's sometimes seemingly cold, hard and superficial world. But the more we can look within and discover our own truth, the more likely we all are to continue our journey through life with an open heart.

Our minds and bodies are intricately connected and I truly hope that as you journeyed through, you felt the shifts both mentally, spiritually and physically. It's my desire that the insights, activities and anecdotes within have resonated with you, gently guiding you towards a deeper understanding of yourself and the world around you.

From the quiet moments of introspection to the invigorating and sometimes uncomfortable revelations of self-discovery, I hope this has served as a steadfast companion, enlightening and empowering you at every turn.

Thank you for allowing me the honour of being a part of your voyage of discovery. I trust that the ripples of transformation you've initiated here will echo through the vast oceans of your life, bringing forth waves of positive change and boundless joy, peace and growth. Above all I hope you find alignment with your physical and non-physical counterpart that is your very soul.

"Mirror, mirror of my soul, enlighten me and make me whole".

With deepest appreciation and warmest wishes,

Ellie Richards

DIGIDOG

"Unleash Your Curiosity: Discovering the World - A DigiDog Series of Books in Honour of Chico, Our Beloved Pomeranian"

Welcome to a new series of books, crafted in memory of our dear pet Pomeranian called Chico. For over 15 years, he continued to delight us with his never-ending curiosity, constantly exploring and investigating everything, everywhere he went.

It is in honour of his spirit of exploration that we present this exciting collection of books that we hope will quench your thirst for knowledge and spark your imagination.

In the series, you will embark on a journey of fascinating people with unique life stories, intriguing subjects and the mysteries of the world. Each book provides a number of carefully researched and thoughtfully curated facts that are designed to surprise, enlighten and entertain you.

From the depths of the ocean to the heights of the sky and beyond, our books will transport you to new worlds and reveal the wonders that lie within them. Join us on this adventure and let Chico's legacy inspire you to never stop exploring and learning.

The DigiDog series includes books for both children and adults.

END

9 785406 042168